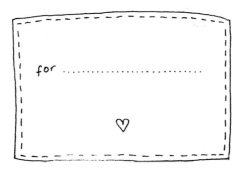

· LOVE NAMES ·

"there is no remedy for love but to love more"

-thoreau-

"love me...

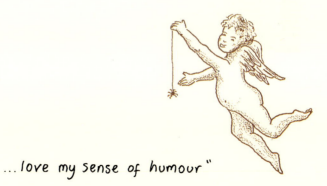

...love my sense of humour "

will you be my valentine?

GREAT PARTNERSHIPS · Nº 1

FOOD FOR LOVERS

strawberries

champagne

oysters

honey

dates

nasturtiums

caviar

cream

mango

GREAT PARTNERSHIPS Nº 2

♡· KISSING WITH CONFIDENCE ·♡

(i) Clean teeth until they sparkle
(No fragments of spinach or garlic breath)

(ii) Relax and move closer

(iii) Close eyes and pucker up

(iv) Enjoy!

"love me...

...love my dog"

"in the arithmetic of love
one plus one equals everything
and two minus one equals nothing"

· mignon mc laughlin ·

GREAT PARTNERSHIPS Nº 3

"love me...

... love my work"

GREAT PARTNERSHIPS Nº 4

sometimes you're a......

cuddly teddy bear

sex bomb!

ray of sunshine

sometimes you're a......

prickly cactus

cold fish

sack of potatoes

"love me...

... love my friends"

island paradise

sun... sea... sand...

"there is only one happiness in life, to love and be loved"

· george sand ·

when you're in love...

the world turns upside down

GREAT PARTNERSHIPS Nº 5

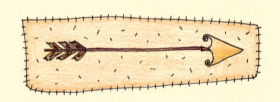

"love me...

... love my dancing."

GREAT PARTNERSHIPS Nº 6

"love me...

...love my habits"

"of all the gin-joints in all the world.... you had to walk into mine"

GREAT PARTNERSHIPS Nº7

"love me...

... love my singing'

LOVE SICKNESS

loss of appetite

day-dreaming

racing heart

lack of concentration

childish behaviour

mood swings

GREAT PARTNERSHIPS N°8

· I love you even when you're angry ·

"love me...

... love my hairstyle"

together we can

sail across the clouds...

catch moonbeams...

slide down a rainbow...

· moonbeam ·

GREAT PARTNERSHIPS Nº 9

"love is like the measles:
we all have to go through it"

jerome. k. jerome

I'd like us to grow old together...

"love me...

...love my driving"

I
want
to
share
everything
with
you
♡

GREAT PARTNERSHIPS Nº 10

"love me...

...love my mess"

I wear my heart on my :

sleeve

pocket

lapel

trouser leg

shoe

hat

GREAT PARTNERSHIPS Nº11

I want the world to know how much I love you...

"love me...

love my little fibs!"

heart shaped things

　petal

　strawberry

　leaf

GREAT PARTNERSHIPS Nº 12

"love me...

...love my daydreaming"

· a little message ·

GREAT PARTNERSHIPS Nº 13

"love me...

...love my impatience"

we fit!

GREAT PARTNERSHIPS Nº14

"love me...

...love my cooking"

you're just right!

GREAT PARTNERSHIPS Nº15

"any time that is not spent on love is wasted"

·tasso·

"Adding a sprinkling of magic to the everyday"... is how Lauren White describes her original style of drawing. Born and brought up in the Bedfordshire village of Cranfield, she studied fine art in Hull and London before returning to Bedfordshire to work as resident illustrator for a local wildlife trust. She loves playing the piano, walking her dog, Jack and carries a sketchbook everywhere she goes. She lives with her partner, Michael, and describes herself as having an astonishing collection of marbles and a wicked sense of humour. Lauren's designs for Hotchpotch greetings cards are sold around the world and in this book she continues to refine her dinstinctive style which "celebrates the simple things in life."

Published by MQ Publications Limited
254-258 Goswell Road, London EC1V 7EB

Copyright © MQ Publications Limited 1998

Text & Illustrations © Lauren White 1998

ISBN: 1-897954-07-7

1 3 5 7 9 0 8 6 4 2

All rights reserved. No part of this publication may be reproduced or transmitted in any form or by any means, electronic or mechanical, including photocopy, recording, or any information storage and retrieval system now known or to be invented without permission in writing from the publishers.

Printed and bound in Spain